20 Day Budget Challenge for Couples

Build Profitable Money Habits and Watch More Money Dance in Your Wallet

Table of Contents

Publisher's Note

The publication is designed to provide accurate and authoritative information regarding the subject matter covered. It is sold with the understanding that the publisher is not engaged in rendering psychological, financial, legal, or other professional services. If expert assistance or counseling is needed, the services of a competent professional should be sought.

For Bowen,

my extraordinary partner in life and work

Day 1: Why Budget?

Most of us learned this in a hard way

"Why me, God? Why me, huh? I don't even deserve to be in this situation. I deserve to be more. Why is it me? Why have you done this to me?"

Sounds familiar, right? It's like when you just received a large bill when you found you didn't save enough money by the end of the month for a trip. You and your spouse spent too much and just found out you two have to postpone your family trip due to lack of budget…

Once in a while, my family's financial condition was also in such an embarrassment, that we had to save up every penny at the end of the day for our kids so we can have enough money to pay our mortgage and all the bills. Weird! We calculated that we had enough income to cover these and still could have some left to spend on here and there, we just didn't know where "the rest" went! It was just gone! I didn't see any way out by that time. Despite the diligent work of my husband and me, there was still nothing left after we paid all the necessary costs. I was overwhelmed with humiliation, anxiety, and guilt. I still remembered the shame of asking my parents for some "assistance," so we can have some savings to take our kids out for a holiday meal. Also, we were afraid of answering the call, because we assumed that a creditor could be on the line.

End of my story, the financial struggle of a young couple at that time.

Maybe you've been on your own for a long time since you've done all right financially. But things become different when it comes to both of you, you and your partner, even with one or several kids around. All kinds of spending will come up, some you really need, and some come as a surprise. If you don't have a budget and plan ahead of time, those numbers will eventually be out of control. You will say, "Oh, it actually much more than I thought in the first place!" Yes, for yourself, you know there's a better way to handle your money. To get things under control this time for "our money," you will need to get familiar with yourself, your partner, your kids, and your life as a family. It will help you make sure that you can make it work all the way to and beyond retirement.

On the other side, you might be lucky enough not to be in a deep financial hole. You may have seen people struggling in debt — your parents, neighbors, or friends. You might know enough about it to stop it yourself, you may have graduated from college early, or you have a smart wife or husband. He is really good at taking care of this. Perhaps the only reason you picked up this book is to learn the right way to set up your budget and manage your finances, especially when it comes to the lives of both of you.

It doesn't matter why you picked this book up. What is significant is that you have taken a critical step in developing an increasingly expensive habit — the budgeting habit (Griffiths, et al., 2020).

Day 2: We Want A Bigger Life!

What's in your mind about budgeting?

It's hard to survive without a budget. While you may have felt the opposite way — that living on a budget is hard. I know you have tried hard to avoid the b-word because when you hear or even think of the word "budget," you just wish that I could stop here.

- "The budgets are restrictive."
- "You can't have fun because you're on a budget."
- "I'm not going to give up my rights...Ah... I still want a new headphone next month, so I'm going to keep my budget.
- "It's too hard to have a budget!!

Okay, I know how much we hate the word. Would you think life was fun when your phone rang several times a day because you didn't pay the bills? Does it feel comfortable when your electricity is cut off? How about when you had to tell the landlord that you didn't have enough money to pay the rent this month? Does all of that sound like fun experiences?

Let me tell you about myself

Let me tell you, it's certainly not, not to say that you are living with your partner, and your kids, you certainly don't want them to take the same pain.

I've told the sad story of myself when I was young, then what happened after me and my husband started to realize it was time to change?

Things are different for us because we realized there's actually a way out when it comes to the financing of a family or a couple. No matter how deep your financial hole, you will crawl out. Once we started to work on a budget, we began to take our life back little by little. We first started with clearing out all our debt, then got control overspending, and paid off our mortgage….yes, just little by little, but we made it. I left my job a few years ago, and now I'm working from home, doing what I love. We paid cash for our daughter's wedding, we travel several times a year, big travels! We also spend a few months out of the year visiting my elderly mom and also working in a more relaxed environment and pace. And the list can still go on.

Now you tell me — is life better with or without a budget?

Day 3: Meet Yourself in Future

Challenges in budgeting

Now both of you have seen what a different budget can make to my life. Let's jump into the "How." Although living on the budget can make you feel safer and more predictable than all surprises and chaos without a budget, there are still some struggles and challenges, especially when you just start to set it up. Here are some everyday things we feel challenged in budgeting, among all those we surveyed, distributed by percentages:

- Unexpected costs (22 %)
- Resisting such impulse purchases-(19 %)
- Monitoring their purchases-(16%)
- To be consistent with the budgeting habit-(16%)
- Handling budgets for friends and relatives (mainly spouses) -(13 %)
- Not understanding how to budget-(6%)
- Generating small or sporadic income-(6%)

If you find yourself fall into debt again with an unexpected cost, buy stuff impulsively at the checkout line, or feel ashamed when a friend tries to undermine your efforts? You're not alone!

The good news is, none of these obstacles is unsolvable. Here we're going to teach you how to resolve all of the financial hurdles you're currently facing by setting up budgets for both of you and your family. You can no longer feel powerless in the world of finance, which makes you and your partner feel stressed and helpless, even just talking about it. Rather than allowing your money to rule your family life, you must believe that you will eventually become the master of money.

We need to have dreams.

Imagine the future of your life will help accelerate budget setups (Cheema & Bagchi, 2011).

Let's just pause for a second, imagine what your life would be like a year from now, five years from now, and perhaps ten or more years after both of you have developed a perfect budgeting habit. Discuss each other and picture that out.

What does it look like? Does it look like that you're no longer in debt? Maybe you can travel several times a year together? Or you may have saved enough, so you are planning to get a bigger house for your kids to play around? Even the money you now pay to credit card companies will be spent on repairing your home, taking a holiday, or saving in your retirement fund? How does it feel like when you can enjoy your holidays without worrying about your credit card, which is likely to come in next week?

When two of you walk into the furniture shop with a reasonable budget in place, you'll know exactly how much you have to spend on a new sectional or dining table. You'll enjoy buying it without being guilty. You will have some significant life events to spend money on, such as your child's college or wedding, or a down payment for the first house. With a budget plan, no problem, you've planned ahead, and you can pay cash right here, right now.

Financial freedom is not just for the most one or two wealthy people. It's for regular people like you and me. And it all begins with a simple budget setup. Imagine the day when you have all the finances under control, making purchases and investment, and living the life of your dreams.

Tell me something about you

Take a few minutes to think about and answer the following questions:

- Have you tried budgeting before? If so, how did it go?

- What type of resistance do you feel when you think about budgeting?

- Are you willing to go all-in with developing the budgeting habit?

- How does the thought of being in control of your finances make you feel?

A walkthrough on what to expect in the next

How to create a budget and keep It? I will put it in a straightforward way for you to master the budgeting habit so you won't ever worry about what's going on with your family finance.

You will learn the tips below:

- The first few steps to build an applicable budget, and what to do if you have more expenses than incomes of both of you

- Five different approaches to budgeting, and how to decide which one is the right one for you

- How to tap into your deeper motivation, and stick to your budget when you want to quit the plan

- How to build small and practical financial goals will bring you a bigger picture of your business dreams

- How to turn those financial goals into habits, so you can hit the targets without a lot of tension and stress

- How to create an environment for both of you to stick to your budget without failure

- Three accountability approaches to keep you on track

- How to get out of debt fast, save for a down payment or a wedding, or increase retirement fund contribution

Budgeting is the first step towards mastering your finances, let's start this journey to develop this vital habit.

Start to make your dream come true

First, commit yourself to the process of forming the budgeting habit with wholehearted. Let go of any previous financial mistakes or stresses. See today as a new day, a fresh start with your commitment will take that nonsense away and make yourself dedicated.

Second, it doesn't matter whether your writing is good or bad, writing gives you a clear picture of where you are now. It provides a record of your budgeting journey that you can always turn to when you need it.

Both of you have answered 4 questions about your budgeting experiences. Put them down in a notebook. Keep the journal clear and tidy, because you'll use it in the coming chapters as well.

Day 4: Money Grows on Trees

The compounding effects

When you just start to set a budget for the first time, it will not appear to make much of a difference. In fact, maybe there are some frustrations here. You might feel like you've got less money than you did to spend, compared to when you weren't budgeting. But don't get beaten down from the start, just like both my spouse and I have experienced: small habits can contribute to some massive results.

For example, saving $4.00 per day might not sound like a big deal, but with good budgeting habits, even if you are a person with a low income, you can still save at least $120 or more in a month, yes, just $4.00 in a day.

Here are a few things you can do with $120 a month, and there are more you can think of:

- Put it in a Holiday fund. You'll have $1,200 to spend over in the holiday season without getting the annoying credit card bill in January.

- After one year, you will have over $1,400 to buy some large appliances, such as refrigerators or washers and dryers.

- Create an emergency fund to deal with emergencies such as vehicle repairs.

- Place this $120 a month into your savings account. After 30 years, you'll have over $88,000 at a 5% annual interest rate. Obviously, that's not enough to quit your job, but it's a big step in the right direction with such a small monthly saving.

We see the lesson now, while $120 a month might not seem like much, there's a lot you can do with this money if you commit to saving a little of it every day.

The harmful compound effect from mismanagement

There are many significant compounding effects of using the budget to manage and nurture your money well. The negative impact of non-budgeting habits can also be compounded over time. Think of how most of us spend on things—put it on a credit card. Let's say you have a credit card balance of $5,000 with an interest rate of 15 percent, if you choose to pay $100 a month, it will take 79 months for you to pay off. And that's assuming there's no extra charges or punishments! The $5,000 ends up to be $7,900 in total.

See how a non-budgeting habit can cause a negative compounding effect?

Also, there are some other problems you will have to deal with when you have a negative compounding effect. You won't have extra savings to afford holiday and birthday gifts for your partner and your kids. Your credit card balance will start to crank up, so will the interest

.

- Creditors will give you a call.

- Driving an old car that always breaks down

- Don't have time to plan for any romantic events for your partner.

- Feel insecure and fearful when you lose jobs or start retirement.

Time for questions!

You've read this far, here are some questions for you two, don't forget to discuss your answers and put them onto the notebook:

- For the $120 savings per month, what's your choice? If you had to pick just one thing to do with an extra $1,400 a year?

- Was there a specific incident in your past where financial mismanagement caused you or your partner embarrassment?

- How has a lack of budgeting impacted those you love, such as your partner and your children?

- Have you ever calculated the actual cost of your credit card debt?

Let's go from here

Next, write in your notebook to illustrate how budgeting is going to change your life, your partner's lives, and your whole family. Don't be afraid to have a huge dream! Because what you are writing down is essential to motivate you to execute your plan:

- Is there a place you've always wanted to go to?

- What about the gifts that you would like to give to your children and your partner?

- Do you think of buying a house or renovating your existing home?

- How about putting your kids to college, debt-free?

- Do you ever dream of early retirement?

Now, grab a piece of paper and write down an embarrassing financial event you two have experienced in the past. It may be anything from lending money to cover some bills, creditors calling, or even your children being humiliated by wearing old shoes on the first day in school. Make sure to explain how you feel at that moment.

Then, crumple up the paper and throw it out. Visualize that you are throwing away all the old days, and you will start to live a new life from now on.

Great job, now it's time to write down your future reality as though it had already happened. For example, write down something like taking your kids to shop for new clothes and expensive trending shoes and how comfortable you feel when you pay for them without going into debt. Describe their enthusiasm when they got them. This is something you're looking forward to happening, instead of writing it on a piece of paper, writing it down in your notebook this time, to keep this on record.

After that, try to make amends to those you hurt (maybe your partner or parents) due to mismanagement of your finances. Apologize and pray for forgiveness. If you don't have a way to communicate in person, write a letter or leave a short message.

Finally, pick a thing that you would like to buy in the future when you get that far, such as a new refrigerator or a big piece of furniture. Compare the cost of paying cash to use a credit card with three or five years to pay off the item.

Day 5: Know Your "In and Out"

Start by gathering things up

First, you need to calculate the actual amount of your total revenue as a couple and add up all the debt and mandatory expenses. I know it is always a terrifying thing to do things you have never done before. I still recall how much pain this caused us when my partner and I eventually agreed to face all these numbers regarding our financial situation. So, put on some comfortable clothes with your favorite music, and grab a drink of your choice (don't accidentally get yourself drunk!).

When you're single, you can do this on your own. Still, now you're in a relationship with shared finances. Commit ahead of time not to point fingers at your partner for any less-than-ideal aspects of your financial situation. This is new to you both. Either way, it's better to know than not.

You just need a small number of things to get started:

- Create a spending spreadsheet on your laptop. You can also write on a piece of paper to clearly look at what is what.

- List your income for the past 12 months. This may be in the form of check stubs or deposit records in your bank account(s).

- Credit card and bank statements for all accounts as detailed as you can.

Now, how much money do we make?

Write down all your sources of revenue. Be sure to include anything that you both contribute (and maybe some from your family regularly).

Let's now measure your monthly income. If your income remains the same every month, this is a simple move. Only using the sum of your monthly household income. If your spouse's salary varies every month, then measure your average monthly household income by adding up your total monthly income for the past 12 months and dividing it by 12.

Not bad, then how much money did we spend?

Now, let's see what are expenses by categories, sounds time-consuming, and it is. This may be the scariest part when you find out you spend so much only on ice creams or dine outs. But it's also an important step to help us move forward, so don't miss this step or miss the numbers you will include here. It's not the time to beat yourself up, but it's the time to face the truth of where your money has gone over the last few months. This allows you to decide how much you can put into specific categories within your budget, and where you need to cut back to keep your budget.

Go through your credit card and bank account statements, and write down all your expenses for at least the last three to six months, clarify numbers and categories accordingly. You may look at your bank statement and find that last month you spent $200 on grocery stores in the first week, then $150 on the second week, $170 on the third week, and $280 on the final week, totaling $800 on grocery stores! You can also find that last month you spent a total of $350 on restaurants, $70 on movies, $160 on your energy bill, and so on.

Ideally, it's good to go back to look into the scope of a whole year. Looking back on the numbers from the past year will give you a more detailed view. Also, watch for major but non-frequent spending, such as holidays spending, birthdays spending, and home and car maintenance costs regularly.

Day 6: The "Split-Run"

Introduction of the "split-run"

It is a scary but a significant move in our process. Take numbers of one month at a time, and prepare to take a break and get up for a walk, don't let yourself be too stressful. Indeed, some of you feel overwhelmed by the thought of spending a whole day writing down your expenses. That's totally understandable. You can use the "split-run" technique to do this. Whenever you're dealing with a large and complex project, all you need to do is split it into small chunks. Like most people, divide a tedious and long marathon into multiple short runs to achieve it. Unfortunately, many people just don't apply this strategy to their lives. Since most of the time, we are forced to deal with big projects when our boss calls us and says he will need this by the end of 12PM. Not cool at all! So we tend to delay or even entirely neglect them because it is a marathon, boring, long, and no way we can chill down to think about how to do it.

So this "split-run" is built to overcome this kind of "not cool moments" that we all experience when asked to finish a potentially unpleasant and lengthy task. You know it has to be completed, but you just don't pull the trigger, because it sounds just like a marathon to run. So the goal here is to split this 10-hour job into five to ten minutes a day. It is the best way to deal with this budgeting process that you can write down all your expenses and break them into some day-to-day tasks. And in twelve days, you're going to see everything on your spreadsheet for the last year.

Give each other a thumb up if you both get it, and you are ready to dive into it!

Day 7: Act

We just told each other we are ready to go. Great, let's take the spreadsheet, writing down detailed expenses for 5 main categories if you find this makes sense to you and your family:

Monthly mandatory expenses

Those are the costs that you believe are most necessary for both of you. There are no correct or wrong answers to what our priorities are. Everyone has a different preferable lifestyle, but just to make sure these are things that you really have to pay for every month. Here are a few things from my budgeting plan in this category:

- Mortgage for the house
- Tuitions for homeschooling
- Gas
- Gasoline
- Water supply
- Home, car and health insurances
- Electricity
- The Internet
- Grocery
- Interest and taxes
- Water sewer bill for the house
- Amazon prime

True costs

Actual costs come up less often in one or two months (maybe half a year), but that will be things you might want to save up regularly so that you have the money available when you need it. For instance:

- Maintenance of the vehicle and our home
- Health care
- New clothes and diapers maybe
- Stuff for holidays, birthdays, birthdays, marriages, etc.
- Snow cleaning on the roof (unless you can do it)
- Newspapers and subscriptions
- Savings and investments of your own choice

Payments for debts

I know, this is something the worst in this list, now we're trapped in a debt-based world. And, unfortunately, a significant portion of your budget would be spent on debt payments like:

- Student Loans;
- Self-loans like mortgage and cars
- Late fees and interests for credit cards
- Wedding loan if applicable

Investment for quality of life

Here comes one of the most significant investments you can make for yourself and your family. We believe that we would do our best to invest money in a few places like:

- Romantic dinners
- Short trips all together
- Gifts for holidays
- Fitness
- Education (not only for kids!)
- Long term savings for something nicer

Even more fun experiences

Eventually, all that money does is to give you a better life that you want. So, let's consider putting some money aside just for fun experiences to enrich your family's life. Those fun activities may include:

- Eating out whenever you think it's time for a celebration on some milestones.

- Spending on some "quality time" away from the children, only between you two

- Gaming if you like it but doesn't make your partner angry

- Music of your choice

- Movies (not on your phone, but in somewhere like AMC)

Sum up your expenses now

Now it's time to sum up, your expenses and determine what you pay on average per month. Take a look at the final column or row on your spreadsheet to see how much you put on average. Try to get the gross amount of your monthly spending from that.

If you are using a pencil and paper instead of a spreadsheet, here's how to measure your total monthly expenses manually. Just adding up how much you spent every month in each of the following categories you just wrote down on your notebook:

- Monthly target
- True Expenditure
- Interest Transactions Debt Payments
- Quality of Life Resources
- Experiences of leisure

Great job so far!

Few questions for you at the end of this list

- How do you feel seeing all these? Happy or a bit upset? If it's the latter, try to discuss with your partner a bit more, the most important thing is not to see how many of these you can do like a competition, but find a balance in your life. Then we shall look at how much you can spend on in reality.

- Can you divide them into "needs" and "wants"? This will play a significant role in getting your budget under control, do it first on yourself, and we will get to it together in the next chapter.

- Did you sacrifice or hide anything at all when writing this down? If some of those meet the criteria, don't take them off. We need to see everything that can be added into these categories for a comparison with how much money you make to make a final decision.

Day 8: Need or Want?

Differentiate "needs" from "wants"

The first step in managing your budget is to distinguish between "needs" and "wants." For example, paying your electricity and energy bills every month is a must. But going out for lunch every day with friends is not a high priority.

If you use a spreadsheet, but only the necessary items in sheet two. If you are writing on your paper, grab another one just for the essential stuff. It is the budget of your bare-bones. Compare your bare-bones budget with your actual income. If your bare-bone budget precisely matches your income, you are just living. This is definitely noted glamour, but at least you are not overspending. If your bare-bone budget goes beyond your actual income with lots of debt, you need to increase your revenue and reduce it. If your bare-bone budget is much less than your real income, make some fun spending.

See what we can do, with the "not good"

By the way, it rarely happens, but if you find that your bare-bones budget eats up very most of your money you can make, you two even feel breathless to face such a life. It's the time that you need to get out of that situation as soon as you can. You would need to temporarily take an extra job to pay off whatever is eating your budget now, or consider moving to a cheaper home or apartment to speed things up. Each family member has the responsibility to do whatever you can to keep certain items in the budget at a lower amount. For example, if both movies and dinners are high priorities to your partner, ask what matters most — dinner or movies. If both matter equally, discuss if you can lower the frequency, maybe every month rather than a weekly dinner or a weekly movie night. Or you can propose to cook when it comes the time. Then your partner can enjoy a movie from Netflix while you're cooking or after dinner.

In this case, you two may face some painful sacrifices. No need to be too upset, you're not alone that we all have our own problems. In fact, at one of my own downturns, my husband and I, along with our two children, moved from a large home in a vast and quiet neighborhood to a tiny apartment. We had to renew the lease twice a year. I still can remember the pain of that decision, as I got rid of most of our belongings just to fit in that tiny place, for 4 of us.

It's temporary!

Things got a turnaround after the drastic move. Our new budget plan laid the foundation for a new level of financial independence that we still enjoy today. Around a month after that move, my husband and I got new jobs, we have a stable amount of money saved every month. We lived in the apartment for three years, paid off our debt, raised our healthy kids, and kept up our own home.

Time for reflection

Now, you have your "needs" and "wants" in your spreadsheet or the note, let's discuss a few questions together:

- How do you feel about it when you mapped out your income and expenses? Happy or a bit frustrated this time? If you feel depressed looking at this, then you've known that budgeting is a way to tell yourself the truth about your financial condition. Learning the truth is the first step toward financial independence.

- What are those things you both agreed to spend money on, and how much? Needs vs. wants?

- If you have more expenses than your income, what commitments can you make to balance things out from now?

Let's recap the keys and move forward.

Let's briefly recap the process of figuring out your expenses and income, in details:

- Get all you need on your hands, such as a spreadsheet, paper and pen, reports of your income and expenses, such as bank statements.

- Sum up all your income, two of you.

- Sum up all of the expenses by category (e.g., food, house payment or loan, electricity, etc.).

- Compare your actual income to your expenses.

Find out if your gross expenses are higher than your income at this moment. If you want to make more rooms to save up for something, differentiate your "needs" from "wants." Remove or compromise unnecessary things so the figures can suit the way you want. Note the sacrifices do not always have to last forever, just like the example I cited of myself.

And for some of us, if you need to temporarily bring in extra cash, brainstorm with your partner to come up with at least five ways to make some fast cash. This can be helpful for you who are not satisfied with how numbers worked out. But no matter how difficult it is, always believe in each other, holding your hands, smiling at each other, and making some plans together. Note that you may feel life is tough if numbers work out bad, but this feeling is natural when you face the reality of your financial situation. Eventually, a good budgeting habits will lead to freedom.

You may have written a lot in your notebook so far. Whether you feel the number works outright or not, let's write down the vision you have on your financial future. How much cash in your bank, how much in your retirement funds, how much positive cash flow per month? Really see it if it were already a reality. Don't be afraid of dreaming big, knowing that your financial condition will change when you begin to treat your money wisely.

Day 9: Find Your Best Way

Pick one that suits you

Let's guide you to pick a specific budgeting model to adopt, that you are now aware of your actual income and expenses (maybe for the first time!). There are dozens, perhaps hundreds, of budgeting strategies – each has its own pros and cons. Having some experience practiced lots of them, here are 5 strategies that I would recommend to take as references:

NO.1. The 50/30/20

This one was Initially introduced by Harvard economist (and current U.S. senator) Elizabeth Warren and her friend, Amelia Warren Tyagi (2005). The 50/30/20 budgeting strategy distributes your net income to the following percentages:

- 50% on needs (e.g., house payment or loan, food, electricity, petrol, car payment)

- 30% on demands (dinner out, movies, etc.)

- 20% savings / investment / payment of debt

The most significant advantage of this strategy is that it offers a balanced approach to ensure that you fulfill your daily needs. However, you will still be able to save for some desires and potential costs.

NO.2. The 80/20

Unlike the 50/30/20 approach, the 80/20 budgeting approach put net income in percentages, although it is a much less comprehensive approach. With this strategy, every time you get paid, put 20% of your net income into savings, and use the remaining 80%. The advantage of this strategy is that it requires little effort and time to execute it and does not require any further deep dives or allocations.

The biggest downside of this approach is that it does not take seasonal expenses and some potential costs into consideration, such as quarterly car insurance payments, Holiday spending, and other things. So, when those come up, you might not have enough "floating money" to cover them, so you will be dipping into your savings account.

This strategy is only recommended for those who are not good at looking into distributed categories and cannot track your expenses. If you take this method, be sure to pay for your essential stuff, such as rent, utilities, and food, directly after you get your paycheck or other payments. You may want to increase your savings percentage to 25-30 percent, so you have enough backups to spend on those "hidden costs," without getting too deep into your savings.

NO. 3. The envelope approaches

With this method, you use cash instead of using a credit or debit card to keep you away from interests and potential costs. After developing your budget based on something like the 50/30/20 strategy, you can divide your cash into some envelopes representing different categories, as you listed in the last chapter. For, e.g., put money for food in the grocery envelope. Once you go to the grocery store, get the cash out of that envelope to pay for the groceries (don't take the wrong one).

The envelope method works well for areas where you have a higher tendency to blow your budget even if you have a budget set up. Such overspending can be in specific categories such as food, shopping, and entertainment. The significant part about this strategy is that when the money is gone in one of the envelopes, you will have to temporarily stop spending in that category. That makes you clearer about your expenses.

But there are a few disadvantages to this one too. For some people, especially those who have lots of stuff to keep, if you can't find any envelopes or some got stolen, your money is gone, literally. Some of us may not want to bring all the cash with you all the time because of that. The envelope method can also be more complicated since we are couples, and only one person may have the cash on hand. We possibly prefer to divide cash into half for each partner or have each other responsible for specific categories. That makes the whole thing more complicated and requires lots of management. Envelopes may also be inconvenient, which is a problem, especially nowadays, when some don't even bring our wallet out there but just use Apple Pay.

Although there are disadvantages to this strategy, it is perfect for those who are struggling with overspending, attempting to get out of debt eagerly or want to strictly manage every expense out of hand.

NO.4. The "zero" strategy

That means that the income minus expenditure will be zero. But don't get me wrong, that doesn't mean you're going to end up with $0.00 in your bank account, but you're going to account for every penny of income and expenses.

The most crucial advantage of zero-based budgeting is that you need to assign every dollar a task. This makes you even more explicit about your expenses. You will keep a tidy and systematic accounting book, and either of you can get to know what is from it clearly without confusion.

The main problem is that because zero-based budgeting is more detailed to conduct, it will take more time than some of the other budgeting approaches.

NO.5. Automation

Many of you may find it beneficial to automate some of the budgeting processes. For example, you can automatically transfer a certain amount of money from your savings account every month or sign up for a spouse investment program. The idea here is to use technology to eliminate much guesswork and improve the decision-making process. Each month, the money will come out of your account and go to different "budget buckets."

The most significant advantage of this approach is that you don't have to make any financial decisions with all that have been set up already.

On the other hand, a big downside is that you may become financially lazy. Once you set it up in the first place, you're going to stop tracking all your spending, don't know exactly where your money is going, or just forget about it gradually. It doesn't sound like a habit in this case.

Or just a combination?

The beautiful thing about these budgeting methods is that you can mix and match them for better fitting in your own situation. For example, you can use the "zero" budgeting strategy with a 50/30/20 budget. You create three broad categories for your finances. In this way, you can also track every dollar in the 50/30/20 to make sure you know where your money is being spent. Or you can combine the budget of 50/30/20 with the envelope strategy, by using cash to pay for items that fall under the 30% (wants) section.

Overall, all of these budgeting strategies can work — either individually or combined. The key to getting them to work for you is to make a plan and commit to sticking to it!

Still, deciding?

Answering some of these questions to help you:

- What was your gut reaction when you read about these budgeting strategies? Do you hear yourself say, "That's the one!" or "No way?"

- How detailed are you two when it comes to your comfort level of budget?

- Do you have a hard time tracking all costs, do you get used to entering details into a spreadsheet or app?

- For those "wants," what are things driving you to spend on those?

- Put answers into your notebook, you can revisit these with your partner to see if there's another way to do these works for you.

Make a move!

It's essential to be transparent with yourself and each other. That's the only way to clearly figure out which type of budgeting method really works the best for you. With that in mind, pick one or two that you think you should stick with.

For example, suppose you and your partner keep everything very detailed. You may want to combine a "zero" budget approach with a 50/30/20 plan.

On the other hand, if you choose to fly by the seat of your pants, the 80/20 budget combined with automation might be your best bet.

And if you tend to bounce checks, the safest choice might be to use the cash envelope program for something other than your key bills.

The primary step here is to select one or a mix of some that fit your personality and need precisely. Now let's dive into how to build the budgeting habit from here.

Day 10: What's Driving You?

What's your goal by doing this?

If you try to develop a budgeting habit only because you think you should, you're likely to struggle with it. You don't have enough motivation to carry this on. To get to your budgeting success, you want to attach your move to a goal or some long-term purpose that is important to you and your family (Baxter & Pelletier, 2020). As sometimes, challenges and problems will come. It's hard to stick to something like daily budgeting for a long time if you don't have a deeper understanding of your goal and your purpose.

The why

This question is for you two: why would you like to develop a budgeting habit?

Let me help you think, maybe some of you would want to develop a budgeting habit to get rid of all your personal debt, okay, why is that important? What's the intention of getting rid of your debt?

Here's what I can think of if I was asked about this:

- Getting rid of debt is essential for us to have money for a dream holiday.

- Without debt, I can have money for long-term savings and retire earlier.

- If I don't have debt, I will have some free money to launch a "side hustle" to replace my work.

Seriously, what's your reason behind the budgeting habit?

One of the most effective ways to connect yourself with the reason for developing a budgeting habit is to realize the pain without having it, like right now. You will have no problem feeling the pain if you are suffering now. If you are not suffering now, think about the past when you didn't have a budget strategy to help you navigate your finances:

- What is your current biggest disappointment with budgeting, or when you tried this but failed in the past? (or the product of not getting a budget)?

- How have you been affected by the lack of a budget?

- What are your most significant financial regrets?

- What are those bad spending habits you want to break?

And about financial independence:

- How would you describe financial freedom?

- How has not budgeting impacted you in the past?

- What impact does the budget have on your life now, how do you see this in your future?

- How far are you willing to go to make your financial dreams a reality?

Economic independence means differently to all of us, and there's never a correct answer to the "why" above. Some of us tend to work until the typical retirement age and have enough money to pay for living expenses and enjoy free-of-stress retirement life. Some of us may choose to buy a big house in the "right" neighborhood. Neither of these motives is right or wrong, so when you explore your more profound meaning, let go of what you think you should do and realize what matters most to you. Put your goals, purposes, and all that you think will drive you to a successful budgeting strategy down to your notebook. Take that with you, and we will explore the "money goal" next!

Day 11: The Money Goal

What is the money goal all about?

There is a difference between goals and habits. The goal is a specific result you want to achieve in your life. Your goal helps you connect you with your purposes and intentions to get to the target and is the transformation you want to experience. A habit, on the other hand, is the day-to-day implementation and execution of the goal. Usually, patterns aren't as glamorous as goals. Still, your everyday habits will eventually decide what level you're going to achieve in life.

If it comes to setting goals, our recommendation is to set smart money goals for each quarter (i.e., three months) instead of a year. You tend to forget your goals at the end of a year. Here are essential criteria for a smart money goal:

- Specific
- Measurable
- Attainable
- Relevant
- Time-bound

Specificity

- Who and what is involved?
- What do you want to accomplish?
- When do you want to do it?
- Where will you complete the goal?
- What might get in your way?

Specificity is important because when you hit these milestones (date, place, and target), you will know that you have achieved your goal.

Measurable

- How much of it?
- How many of them?
- How easy is it?

Measurable goals are defined with precise times, amounts, or other units — virtually anything that measures progress towards a goal.

Setting measurable milestones will make it easy to determine if you have made any progress from point A to point B. Quantifiable goals also help you find out if you're going in the right direction and not.

Achievable

Achievable targets can extend the limit of what you believe is possible. While you feel a goal is reasonable to achieve but will take some effort, they will make you feel full of challenges and obstacles, more than what you can see from some huge target that's hard to get to. The key here is to look at your daily life and set a goal that seems a little beyond your control. This way, even though you fail, you still gain something of significance.

Relevant

Relevant targets reflect on what you really want. These are the exact opposite of some crazy and inconsistent goals. They're in harmony with all those essential things in your life, from success in your career to the future happiness with the ones you love.

Time-Bound

Time-bound milestones have precise deadlines. You are required to produce the desired outcome before the target date. Time-bound goals are challenging but grounding. You can set your target date for today, or you can set it for a few months, a few weeks, or a few years from now. The key here is to establish a deadline that you can reach by working backward and developing habits.

Before I let you try to go with these, here are some examples from myself, that you can take a reference:

- Savings: I will save up $15,000 for a down payment on a home in the next four years. To stay on track with this goal, I'll save a minimum of $350 each month.

- Investing: I will save 10% of every paycheck and invest it in an index fund.

- Tracking: I will spend a minimum of ten minutes each day to find out how to improve by reviewing my budget and entering any transactions for the day.

- Debt Payoff: I will pay off all credit card debt by the end of this year.

- Savings: I will put a total of $3,000 in an emergency fund by October 30th.

What's in your mind about these?

- How do you feel about setting the goal? Is it something you're scared of, or something you're looking forward to?

- So far, anything has changed in your mind about goal setting?

- Have you set up any goals?
- How likely are you going to achieve the goals you set?

- Do you tend to set ambitious goals and then give up?

46

Time to go for it

Please answer these questions above honestly. And now, review what you have learned, reflect with your partner, and write down at least 5 critical financial goals.

Don't worry, you don't have to focus on all of these in this chapter. We will start little by little, so out of the five you write down, choose one to start working in the next 24 hours.

Finally, add a note to your calendar to review your progress on your goal on a weekly or monthly basis. When you complete the first goal, open up a bottle of red wine, then determine which target to concentrate on.

Day 12: Turn Goals into Habits

In the previous chapter, you just created your own money goal and might have already started on one of them! Great for you! As far as habits, even a series of small practices, are the best ways to master one area of your life and achieve your money goals. That's why you should concentrate on quantifying your habits by putting them into comfortable and daily actions that you are and will complete every day, week, or month. When we complete a practice, we achieve a goal!

Here are some types of habits

- Yes or no — Did you complete habits for the day?

- Metric-based — A specific number and quantity to meet your target of the day, or even set limited time to do it.

- Project-based — Milestones where you chip away at a larger goal with a lot of steps.

As we talked about, let's break these into the frequency we want to complete them.

Daily habits

Ask each other: "What can I do every day? "We'll dive deeper into building small habits, and more simple goals in the next chapter. Now, let's focus on what you can do daily to help you achieve one of your goals. First, make sure that your daily habit leads you towards the goal you set. Second, make sure it's practical, here are some examples:

- Before bed, log into credit card accounts and calculate the total of expenses on that day.

- Put receipts for all expenses of the day into an envelope, or just in your wallet.

- Record all expenses of the day.

- Check to see if your budgeting software has recorded everything correctly.

- Reconcile your checkbook.

Maybe weekly and monthly habits also

In addition to your daily budgeting habits, feel free to add a few weekly, monthly, or quarterly habits. These habits can be helpful in a midterm or long-term run, but they are too detailed to do daily. But weekly and monthly habits are just as important as daily activities. So, here are a few more examples that you can look at for more idea:

- When you use the envelope strategy, we talked before, put the cash in the envelopes, and make sure to count it at the end of the week to keep you on the right track.

- Put a certain amount of your income to the associated budget categories of your financial spreadsheet.

- Check your credit card statements for any unnecessary expenses that should be avoided in the next month.

- Call different auto insurance companies to compare to get some lower rates.

There are thousands of things that can be incorporated into your daily, weekly, or monthly habits. The key here is to identify the specific actions that will drive you towards a significant financial goal and incorporate them into your routine as habits regularly.

What do you think?

- Out of the daily habit examples listed above, which one has made you say, "Oh, that's the one!"

- How do you adapt those habits to suit your situation?

- What kind of habit will you likely commit to regularly doing?

- Are there any new budgeting habits that you need to plan weekly, monthly, or quarterly?

Set them up and execute

Create a list of daily habit options that will help you build your budgeting habit. Rank these habits in the order of priority. Commit to doing the top one regularly. Set up your phone or calendar reminders to remind you to make the habit every day.

Next, make a list of the weekly, monthly, and quarterly habits you want to build up. Determine when you're going to do them. For example, my husband and I have our monthly financial meeting on the first Saturday morning of each month. Mark the time on your calendar for these more time-consuming but less frequent events.

Write your daily, weekly, monthly, and quarterly habits and any additional ideas you may have in your journal.

Day 13: The Habit Pile

The habit pile concept

Habit pile? The central concept here is to create a simple routine you're going to do on a daily (or weekly) basis, which involves a set of simple financial habits (Quinn, et al., 2010). That is what the habit pile is. It's not easy to develop new habits, as you've probably heard. You already have daily chores piling up, picking up your kids, or helping your partner with laundry. It may seem difficult to add anything new to your everyday routine. But my experience can tell you that you have enough time to develop a new habit. Still, you can also add hundreds of habits in your busiest day without having any adverse effect on your life, as long as you learn how to do it through steps below:

- Identify those small important habits and write them down to your notebook.

- Group them together into a routine.

- Schedule a specific time each day to complete this routine.

- Use a trigger as a reminder to complete this pile.

- Make it super easy to get started.

Essentially, the goal here is to identify and complete those habits that you know are highly important, by piling them on top of each other. You may start with a few basic but powerful habits and build on them as this routine becomes a part of your day. Some key elements here for creating your habit pile:

- Why do you choose these habits?
- Which order are you supposed to go with?
- How long do you spend on each one per day?

The key is to treat a habit pile as a single action instead of a series of individual tasks. I know this seems like a small thing, but developing a habit needs a lot of elements if you want to stick to it, for example:

- Schedule time for them (a block of time).
- Identifying a trigger for it.
- Planning what you're going to do to complete it.

If you treat each part of a pile as an individual event, you would have to create a collection of reminders and track each one, which could quickly become overwhelming. However, if you view the whole thing as just one practice, it would be easier to remember and complete regularly.

Day 14: Five Steps to Achieve

NO.1. focus one pile at one time

Don't try to get too much into your busy life, especially when it has already made you overwhelmed. Otherwise, you'll just stop and quit the game, when it's finally too hard to deal with all of those. Commit to a few essential habits that only take five to ten minutes to complete in a day. Which can include some of those I mentioned earlier:

- Putting receipts for all expenses of the day, into an envelope, or just in your wallet.

- Reconciling your checkbook.

- Checking your budget (can be in an app or a spreadsheet), before making a purchase to make sure you have available funds for the purchase.

- Recording all expenses of the day.

And don't do these things as specific tasks you set up before (although somehow, they are) since that will make it harder to flow naturally as a "habit." We suggest that you bring them together in a budgeting pile planned for a specific time in the day.

NO.2. Create a trigger for them

Okay, good job so far, now we need to think out some "triggers" that will remind you to complete the pile of habits, not just by phone or calendar in the long run since they will be "habits." A trigger is a signal that includes one of your five senses (sight, sound, smell, touch, or taste) to serve as a reminder to complete a specific action. Triggers are essential because most people cannot remember multiple tasks without just one reminder. So, a trigger could automatically make you react to it by taking action. It's just like that many people use their alarm clocks or mobile phones as a trigger to wake them up in the morning.

A trigger can be a specific time of day.

The trigger for a habit can happens at a particular time each day, like waking up in the morning, eating lunch, or walking through the door after work. It should be an automatic one to let you react to it.

A trigger should be easy to complete.

Suppose a trigger is very challenging that requires you to take some complicated actions. In that case, you will not fully realize the effectiveness of the trigger. Just like even if you exercise regularly, it's a mistake to use it as a trigger because you might occasionally miss a day.

A trigger should be an existing habit.

This is something you do automatically every day, like showering, going to the refrigerator, or sitting down at your desk. This is important because you need to be 100% certain that you won't miss a reminder.

Some examples that I used to drive myself daily

- After taking a shower after work, I'll record all of my expenditures for the day.

- After taking my kids to sleep, I'll check my bank account balance.

- After getting paid, I'll log into my IRA account and put down 10% of my salary.

NO.3. Stop to take a look when it's going wrong.

You may have tried to do budgeting before but struggled and failed. A crucial step is to recognize the rising pitfalls of your setup budgeting system and then redesign the environment to get things right and success. In the past, for my husband and me, dining out was the biggest eater of our money. Thus, food habits at home are essential to us. When it comes to finances, we all have different challenges in our home. But here are some of the most common pitfalls for us to notice and react to them:

- A child who wants and needs lots of things

- Spending money to ease my emotional discomfort

- Impulse spending

- Going shopping and finding some good deals

- Not having money set aside for emergencies like car repairs.

- Can't wait to go for purchase before funds are available

- Allowing some desires to overrule long-term goals

- Spending money eating out when tired and not wanting to go home and cook

- Being unable to save

- Unexpected expenses for my children like a school trip or other opportunity

NO.4. Make your life towards success.

Now that we've been looking at some common pitfalls people tend to encounter. Let's dig into how to build your environment for success to prevent you from falling back into those "bad habits." What you have to do is recognize the problems you are facing and then build an action plan that will keep you from succumbing to these obstacles.

- Keep staples on hand for quick, easy to prepare favorite meals.

- Stick to Netflix where there are no restaurant commercials.

- Put credit cards in the fridge so you can't use them without thawing.

- Avoid those commercials and shopping channels, so you're not tempted to buy unnecessary items.

- Avoid going to shopping malls.

- Create a goal for getting out of debt with your partner, so that you'll be reminded about it every time you log in.

- Save some money each month for unexpected expenses like car repairs.

NO.5. Not too rushed, but baby steps.

Create your daily routine around financial habits that don't take a lot of work, such as tracking your bank account balance. Those are the little wins that generate significant "emotional momentum." They're easy to remember and complete. With every step, you can realize that you are getting closer, on the right track, and move to a higher level.

Everyone knows that these are straightforward things, but that's the point. You want to get going with these "no-brainer" tasks first because this will minimize the risk that you will miss it compared to some other big or complex ones, even though you feel stressed or busy. We recommend that you select habits that are easy to complete — like anything less than five minutes. Then build a pile around these simple ones. Once these are automatically running, then do you have to add more patterns to this routine.

Keep adding these tiny habits to your habit piling routine until you become the expert in handling all kinds of new habit piles later on.

Post-reading questions

- Have you thought about your triggers related to money? What often trips you up and causes you to "break your budget?"
- What is the most natural good budgeting habit you can implement in no time in a day?

- When you've tried budgeting in the past, what was the obstacle by then? Did you struggle with tracking your expenses?

- Up to this point, what is your most common budgeting pitfall, or likely to be?

- Which one of the 5 strategies do you think fits you the best?

Wrap up to get your hands on

It's time to start developing your first set of budgeting habits! To get going, I suggest following the five steps that I have just outlined. For each one, to begin with, it should take no more than five minutes to complete, and the entire pile should be less than 30 minutes, just to give you enough momentum and pattern to carry on.

Remember: the easier it is to complete these tasks, the easier it is to turn them into lifelong habits.

Next, pick a trigger for this budgeting procedure, comfortable but secure enough for you to react.

Third, identify the specific challenges you personally face when it comes to money and budgeting. This may include lots of things, such as: failing to write down your expenses or struggling with overspending issues. Write down each obstacle and then create a detailed plan of how to prevent this scenario.

Then, with your budgeting efforts, take baby steps. But eventually, you're going to scale up and create a substantial thirty-minute habit pile that helps you stick to your budget.

Turn budgeting into an enjoyable process. You'll find it easier to make a change in your current financial condition!

Day 15: Be Accountable

When we have made some progress

One of the keys to successful habit development is to add accountability for every significant goal. It's not quite enough to just make a personal commitment. Achieving something remarkable for you like financial freedom will require a robust action plan and a supportive network to tap into when encountering some challenges and obstacles (Kelliher, et al.,2020). We've known this is true for your career development and your personal improvement. You're less likely to give up when you have someone on the side to cheer for your achievements (or kick you in the butt when you're likely to give up).

There are many ways to be accountable, such as sharing your success on social media pages, or just hanging out with some other couples and telling them about your new progress. On a professional level, for better encouraging us to keep move forward, here are also two strategies we can learn about:

1. Self-accountability

You can create reminders to keep your budgeting going with calendar and phone. You can even put alerts on your phone to remind you when to do some specific activities at certain times. Such approaches are beneficial to help you keep adding new habits into your everyday routine. Sometimes, when we are exhausted after work, we shall cheer each other up as a couple, celebrate little progress, and motivate each other to keep going.

2. In-Person accountability

It is one of the best ways to create accountability for budgeting. You've already got your partner with whom you're doing everything. In Navy SEALs, whatever you do, you will have a partner for every single mission. Since you have someone you can move forward with, you will feel supported and motivated every step of the way.

Alternatively, you may join some active groups on Facebook or other social media platforms. In those groups, you will find a bunch of people who are taking efforts just like you (sounds the same thing as you prefer to have a companion to jog within the morning). You can be part of that group or a team, and you can even reach out to a mentor for some further accountabilities. Many people make a living by helping and motivating other people on the road to changing their habits and achieving their goals.

Good or bad, we need to keep the accountability for making more significant progress.

Be honest about failures

It might be a real war for us to fight to keep our budgeting habits. It's a process that you've been developing over time, not just in a moment. This means you're going to have some slip-ups and rough days. But keep in mind, in some situations, even if you don't track and put down your spending for a few days, it doesn't mean that you're a loser and you failed this war. Instead, it's just a small hiccup on your way to developing a positive and healthy money habit. And still, no matter if they are good and bad, you need to put them into your record. It is not there to judge you but to help you. Even when you fail to stick to the budgeting habits, you're demonstrating a commitment to your budgeting habits by being honest.

A chain of your success

Put a monthly calendar on the wall, and every time you make progress and have some success, draw a big X on that day when you completed it. In this way, if you stick to the habits, you will find yourself developing a performance chain, a visible one that you can see in the morning and cheer with each other.

Our main goal is to recognize that even when we have a day that's less than perfect, we want to maintain that chain of affirmative action. We don't want to have a complete break. You might have a day where you don't do everything you planned for sticking to a budget. But even if you still spend a few minutes reviewing your budget, you can consider that a successful day.

Put down those milestones!

Nobody says that new habits should be annoying. Seeing your "chain" getting longer day after day can be exciting. Take the opportunity to celebrate the successful progress and milestones of your goals together, on top of that. The reward you get is up to you. Still, it's important to enjoy those great moments along the way and give each other hope and motivation, believing that we will eventually get there! (But please do not break your bank for a celebration! I've seen this before, and you won't like it)

Tell me something about you.

- What are some of the biggest challenges you've experienced with accountability?

- How have you ever benefited from accountability?

- Have you ever shared anything for accountability purposes on a blog or YouTube channel?

- What is the most comfortable budgeting habit you can do daily to keep from breaking the chain?

- What are some visual reminders or rewards you will create to keep your motivation level high?

So far, so good, let's a recap:

Pick one of those apps or just on your calendar to track the one daily habit you've decided to focus on. See how far you can go without breaking the chain!

Set up accountability, either in person or online. You can either join a budget-specific group or just keep each other posted, to share your goals so that we can keep you accountable.

Set a milestone, such as checking your bank balance every day for 30 days, and then come up with a way to celebrate when you hit the milestone. Make sure the way you plan to celebrate will not crash with your financial goals.

Finally, set up a token system or other forms of visual accountability, such as a wall calendar or your own blue bottle of happiness.

Day 16: Weekly Reviews

What is a weekly review about?

To stay on track and keep small setbacks from becoming deeply ingrained negative habits, plan to spend 20—30 minutes reviewing all your practices and goals. Begin by celebrating your achieved milestones, both big and small, during your weekly review.

Next, talk about any mistakes you made. Look for some patterns to find any potential obstacles to your success. We all have some accidentally overspending, here and there. Think about it, say you just got off work one day, and several friends of you dropped by for dinner, boom! You blow your budget for once. Or maybe another time your kid has a little baseball game, you'll pick up some fast food and order some take-out for your kid.

When you keep going through the weekly analysis process, you'll also keep finding lots of new habits that turn out to be obstacles in your way of budgeting. Being focused and continually improving on the plan will help you identify, evaluate, and resolve some bad habits so that you can either substitute these with good habits or get rid of those from your life.

When you keep making the same mistakes, ask yourself why. Was the goal set too high for you at this moment? Where there any other barriers?

After this weekly review, ask yourself questions below and write the answers in your notebook:

- If you already have a weekly review set up, what is your process? Is the process working for you?
- How do you cheer and motivate each other on this journey?
- What's going right for now?
- What went wrong?
- How do I prepare for a better next week?

How can we move forward from here?

The first thing you can decide is to think of what to review every week? What questions to ask yourself and each other? What are the resources you will use for your review? And then what will you do as a result of the evaluation?

For example, you might ask each other about how you did that week's budget. Based on the issues or obstacles you have found in your analysis, adjust the spending habits for the coming week. And if things didn't go well, discuss and summarize what made it difficult for you to do better, and what you need to do in the upcoming week to get your milestone hit.

Day 17: Oh Sh*t!

Even if you've built the environment for achieving your goal successfully, there are still challenges and obstacles in your way there. The best way to resolve problems is to predict the challenges and potential issues ahead of time and make an action plan ahead of them.

Here are some typical budgeting challenges and issues shared by participants in our surveys and some approaches to resolve them.

Unplanned expenses

Imagine that things are all humming along with your budget. You've given a job to every dollar. You feel good about it — until you get a bill for some auto insurance, you pay once a year, and it's big! Or until you wake up and feel cold because your furnace or heater went out. You're looking at your budget, and since you didn't expect that, you don't have the money for it, period. Not knowing what else to do, you resort to pulling out a credit card, which only puts you deeper in debt.

It doesn't feel comfortable and predictable when it comes to things like car repairs or the heater going out. You don't know when they are going to happen, or how much they're going to cost you. The easiest and most effective way is to set up an emergency fund to deal with unforeseen costs or add a certain amount to your vehicle repairs and household maintenance budget every month.

Impulse purchases

You're standing in the checkout line at the grocery store, something tiny and attractive as a chocolate bar or a well-designed book (just like this one you are reading) catches your eyes: "It's only $10," Without any hesitates, you buy it, even though it's not in your budget. That's a small purchase, but all those little impulse purchases add up. Now we are talking about something not that small, regularly.

Here are something you can do about it, or to help your partner about it too:

- Focus on the shopping list, and stick to it, period. If something catches your eyes and don't have it on the chart, put it down and walk away.

- Unsubscribe all the shopping related emails from email lists.

- Leave your credit cards at home. Even better, freeze your credit cards in your fridge so that it takes time and effort to access them.

- Avoid shopping with friends who are big spenders.

It's our friends & families!

Speaking of friends, several of our survey participants listed going out with friends as a major obstacle to their budget. Others said that their children's expenses, such as field trips, cheerleading costumes, and other child-related fees, are throwing them off. Many of us will consider family gifts giving and hanging out with friends (usually lots of spending) to be budget busters.

Referring to your list of those categories, for those unpredictable expenses for your children. Add another sub-category of "school expenses" to your budget. Set aside money for those unforeseen, random, but essential costs regularly.

When you find that the expenses are higher than you can live with your budget, explain the scenario to your children, discussing and getting feedback on what matters most. You can also provide them with a fixed amount of money that can be spent per month on sports, clothes, and other items. Teach them how to set a budget too, generally, if they did well, the remaining amount of money will be their bonus.

As for our friends and families, share your budgeting habit journey with them to help them have some preparations or awareness about your change in spending.

When your income is not stable

If you're in a commission-based sales job or self-employed, you're likely to have a fluctuated or seasonal income. You make a lot for a few months, then a lot less or even nothing for another month. This makes set up budgeting habits complicated because it's too hard to calculate the income every month.

The easiest way to deal with a fluctuated income is to calculate the average salary for the whole year. In this way, you can put yourself on a fixed monthly income that is lower than your actual wage for those high seasons. Then every month, regardless of how much or how less you make, always stick to the budgeting habit. When you handle your money this way, you will see a more stably growing bank balance and feel safer and experience less stress.

For those days, we eat out.

It's hard to break the temptation and the mood to eat out, mainly if used to it. The problem is, money spent dining out comfortably adds up and can easily blow your budget. Below are a few ways to reduce the amount of money you spend in restaurants.

- Once a week, do as much prep work as you can, such as de-freeze the meat ahead of time.

- Prepare a double batch of the main dish, and freeze one to use in the future.

- After your dinner, prepare fruits and vegetables for the next day, move meat for the next night's dinner from the freezer to the fridge to thaw.

- Keep staples on hand for quick, easy to prepare meals.

What are your takeaways?
- For all those obstacles listed in this chapter, which one resonated the most with you?

- What have you tried at this point to deal with the obstacle? What has and hasn't worked?

- In what ways have you allowed other people's opinions to impact your finances negatively?

- How often do you make purchases to impress others? Are you willing to let go of that to get your financial house in order?

Go from here

As always, remember to put your answers to questions above into your notebook.

First of all, build your own list of strategies we've mentioned above, that you can use to deal with each of your biggest obstacles. For example, if impulse purchases are your most significant challenge, commit to taking the two steps to get yourself out of it, such as freezing your credit cards.

When your problems are related to other people, such as friends or family, talk to them about your commitment and progress, then ask for their support.

Ask yourself what you would do if you had a significant financial setback, such as one of you suddenly losing the job? What are you going to do to make your life work? What are the things you need to do to adapt to it? Are there any improvements you can make now to plan for a financial crisis just like that?

As always, baby steps on your way to getting there. Be mindful and clear about things that have happened and something that might occur. Always be prepared, always be adaptive.

Day 18: Small Things Add Up

For those times, we are "waiting"

I know you might just have a few minutes to work on your budget habits daily, we still recommend that you do something about it. The idea here is to use those short pieces of time to actually make some changes in your life.

In addition to any day-to-day habits you have developed. You will improve, maximize some of your short pieces of time to make some steady progress day by day, towards your goals, like when you are waiting for your food is ready from the oven, the time you take to drive to work. Even the time you are waiting outside the door for your take-out. Sure, indeed, you're not going to have the same effect using those little pieces of time as when you spend more significant portions of time. Still, at least you have some time to do something, it is small, but it is better than nothing, right?

There are still lots of things you can do with it, here are some examples and welcome to add more with your partner onto your notebook:

- Check your bank balance, your spreadsheet, or your budget app on your phone before making a purchase.

- Download the Amazon Kindle app (Oh, you have got it already), and load it up with personal finance books to read whenever you have a few spare minutes.

- Review your goals regularly and make sure your actions are reflecting these outcomes.

- Check all your financial statements to make sure there are no unauthorized and surprising charges.

It's so easy to let those spare and small amounts of time slip away from your life. We always assume that nothing remarkable can be done in just five or ten minutes. However, suppose you convince yourself to take some actions as much as you can. In that case, you can use it to achieve something much higher than you think in the long run, just like the compound effect we talked about at the beginning of this book.

Reflection questions

- What do you typically do when you're stuck in the subway station, or sitting around waiting for something or someone?

- What finance-related goals can you accomplish in less than ten minutes?

- Are there any finance books you'd like to read but doubt you don't have time for?

Remember, time is money, so do those small pieces of time!

Starting from tomorrow, you should be aware of all the wasted moments when you're sitting around doing nothing, waiting for your buddy to meet you at the gym, sitting at the doctor's office, or waiting to pick up your kids from school. Put them down in your notebook, talk about it with each other, and figure out how to use them, as a part of your habits.

Day 19: Always Challenge Yourself

Suppose you think so far, you've got most out of this book and had some progress and achievements in your budgeting journey, not too fast, keep reading. You will know how to supercharge your growth and make it even more successful (Sides & Cuevas, 2020). In that case, we will introduce some personal challenges for you if you can do it.

NO.1. Place yourself on a temporary freeze on spending.

I know you probably feel overwhelmed by debts or tired of how long it takes to save for a big financial goal like a new car. To speed up this process, try to freeze spending in one or more categories for a certain amount of time to see if you can. You may go as far as spending money on nothing but basics, such as food, utilities, and rent for a whole year.

If this sound too extreme, consider just starting with a short freeze on some spending. For example, try to skip your morning Starbucks coffee on your way to work, for a week.

To begin with, it doesn't matter how long or short your spending is going to freeze. All it matters is the attitude and goal you have when you apply this. Try to challenge yourself to do this more often (but we are not saying you should not spend). Someday it will pay off in a colossal way! Maybe you will have your new car in just several months!

NO.2. Level up by increasing savings & investments

Some people don't put money into savings or investment accounts, never, because they believe they can't afford it. Well, maybe it's right for them, mainly if your bills are high and your income is low, or you have so much debt that you need to leverage every single penny you make now. But even if you feel like you can't afford to save or invest, make a small commitment like $5 a week — or even a month if needed. The next week or month, you will raise the amount to $6, then $7, then $8, and so on. As you continue this process, it will grow big, at least someday (remember our compound theory in chapter 1?).

If you have already reached a certain level of success in budgeting, try to challenge yourself by putting a certain amount of money aside for other investments. It's always great to have multiple sources of income.

NO.3. The "side hustle."

The trick for this one is to find opportunities to bring in extra money. And always add it to your big goal whenever you find yourself having saved a certain amount of extra money. Many people make extra money by selling items they got from different marketplaces, on eBay or Craigslist, or some people take seasonal jobs to make some extra bucks.

If you get stuck, then I suggest generating income through a tactic that is widely known as a "side hustle," a part-time job that could turn into a full-time income. But the downside for side hustling is, it will drain your spare time with your family, and make you feel exhausted without making too much more. That's why you need to find a side hustle that fits within your time and monetary restrictions.

You know you always want more.

- Do you feel that it's impossible to save enough money for a down payment on a home or retirement?

- What other financial dreams do you have but feel out of reach?

- Which of the ideas for scaling up with personal challenges impressed and resonated with you the most?

- How can implementing at least one of these ideas impact your progress on getting out of debt, or saving up your financial dreams?

Fruits for thoughts

It's time to supercharge your progress towards your financial goals. You're going to do so by adapting at least one of the personal challenges outlined in this chapter.

Let's start by getting out of your notebook and being honest with each other about any discouragement you may feel in finance.

Next, take a look at the list of content in this chapter, and select one challenge that fit yourself, to implement this week.

For example, you might not be able to live without buying clothes for the entire year, but you're willing to cut all the eating outs for the whole week.

Calculate how much money you're going to save with this one change. Determine what you're going to do with the money you're about to save, maybe for something like increasing your investments and paying off more debts?

The goal here is to prioritize money-saving habits and stick to them as much as possible.

Be sure to keep track of all the money you have saved, the extra money you make, and the long-term effect for this, maybe you can draw a much better picture with these changes you made.

Day 20: Keep Rolling!

I'm so glad about the efforts you have made so far! Look at the progress you have made. Look at your footprints on the calendar and the confident smile on your face at this moment! Give each other a high five, grab a drink to celebrate your achievements throughout this 20-day challenge!

Okay, time is up, let's keep rolling... for the next 20 days, yes, budgeting is a life-long habit and journey. You will always repeat, improve, repeat, and improve, to make yourself better day after day!

Let's review the action steps you two have taken at the end of each chapter. See if any further improvements you can make, any rooms for you to make more significant progress in the next cycle, just go for it.

And don't forget what life you want to live on, your reasons for taking this budgeting journey. What your financial dream looks like… they can all be found in your notebook, that I hope you two wrote a lot in it for you to track down.

Get lost in your writings? No worries, as I said, this is a life-long journey. Always repeat all the strategies and suggestions we have in this book. Do it again, approach things in a better way, and make more significant improvements!

Finally, as we bring this book to a close, we want to remind you again that developing the budgeting habit is a journey, a lifelong journey (sorry about the repeat). Your initial budgeting doesn't have to be perfect, and it will take time before you see any significant results. But follow the step-by-step guide that we've presented in this book. We can make sure that your financial future will be brighter than the current one you have right now. I believe it has been a thrilling 20-day challenge so far, always be mindful, always practice, and always aim for something greater!

Thank you so much for reading!

Thank You!

Congratulations on getting through this whole 20-day challenge. You could have picked from dozens of books on setting up budgets, but you took a chance and checked out this one. We believe you've made a great choice!

If you find this book helpful, please take a moment, leave a review, and share it with your friends. Your suggestions and satisfaction are the greatest motivation for our efforts now and in the future.

We feel honored to have put our best efforts to support you and your partner on this beautiful journey!

Reference

Baxter, D., & Pelletier, L. G. (2020). The roles of motivation and goals on sustainable behavior in a resource dilemma: A self-determination theory perspective. *Journal of Environmental Psychology*, 101437.

Bradshaw, J., & Morgan, J. (1987). *Budgeting on benefit: the consumption of families on social security* (No. 5). Family Policy Studies Centre.

Cheema, A., & Bagchi, R. (2011). The effect of goal visualization on goal pursuit: Implications for consumers and managers. *Journal of Marketing*, *75*(2), 109-123.

Griffiths, R., Wood, M., Bennett, F., & Millar, J. (2020). Uncharted territory: Universal credit, couples and money.

Kelliher, F., Murphy, M., & Harrington, D. (2020). Exploring the role of goal setting and external accountability mechanisms in embedding strategic learning plans in small firms. *Journal of Small Business and Enterprise Development*.

Quinn, J. M., Pascoe, A., Wood, W., & Neal, D. T. (2010). Can't control yourself? Monitor those bad habits. *Personality and Social Psychology Bulletin*, *36*(4), 499-511.

Sides, J. D., & Cuevas, J. A. (2020). Effect of Goal Setting for Motivation, Self-Efficacy, and Performance in Elementary Mathematics. *International Journal of Instruction*, *13*(4).

Warren, E., & Tyagi, A. W. (2005). *All your worth: The ultimate lifetime money plan*. Simon and Schuster.